TWENTY-TWO FANTASTICAL FACTS ABOUT DOLPHINS

Stuff you didn't know you didn't know

Justin Gregg

Outside the Lines Press

Twenty-Two Fantastical Facts about Dolphins

© 2015 Justin Gregg

Outside The Lines Press

www.outsidethelinespress.com

ALL RIGHTS RESERVED
This book contains material protected under International and Federal Copyright Laws and Treaties. Any unauthorized reprint or use of this material is prohibited. No part of this book may be reproduced or transmitted in any form or by any means, electronic or mechanical, including photocopying, recording, or by any information storage and retrieval system without express written permission from the author / publisher.

ISBN-13: 978-0-9949240-0-1

DEDICATION

For Ma. You'd have liked this one.
It's much funnier than that other one.

ACKNOWLEDGMENTS

This book exists due to the kind indulgence of my wonderful wife Ranke, and the occasional tolerance of my equally wonderful daughter Mila – who sometimes allows me to stop pretending to be Harry Potter, Obi Wan, or Pinkie Pie just long enough to get some writing done.

Thanks also to Angus MacCaull for imposing a deadline that helped prevent this book from being published in 2036, and for his countless editorial insights. Thanks goes out to the excellent community of writers, editors, and designers in Nova Scotia who helped along the way, and to the arts community in the town of Antigonish who are always happy to lend their support when needed.

This book was made possible with generous support from Earth Touch, Terramar Productions, and the Dolphin Communication Project. Outside the Lines Press would like to thank our sponsors for their total awesomeness.

CONTENTS

Preface
1

Strange Behavior

Dolphins don't drink water
8

Dolphins don't chew their food
13

Dolphins don't sleep
17

Dolphins almost never drown
22

Dolphins beach, and nobody knows why
26

Impressive Skills

Dolphins have super crazy healing powers
34

Dolphins use tools
38

Dolphins carry weapons
41
Dolphins fight in human wars
44
Dolphins sense magnetic fields
49
Dolphins can see your bones
53
Dolphins can hear each other's thoughts
56

Bizarre Anatomy

Dolphins have ears in their jaws
62
Dolphins sometimes have backward dorsal fins
66
Dolphins communicate with their nostrils
69
Dolphins are covered in scars
72
Dolphins are hard to count
75

Messy Relationships

Dolphins kill their own calves
82
Dolphins often die young
86
Dolphins never leave their friend's side
90
Dolphins eat each other
94
Dolphins call each other by name
98

PREFACE

Hello there fellow dolphin-lovers! So I am guessing that you probably know a thing or two about dolphins already. You probably know that dolphins are mammals and not fish. Or that they are playful, intelligent, and altogether charming animals. But I expect that even the most dolphin-crazed among you will find heaps of trivia-nuggets within these pages that will surprise you.

This book is a lovingly curated collection of weird, unexpected, and remarkable bits of dolphin science trivia. I've assembled twenty-two of my favorite dolphin-science facts, many of which I regularly break out at parties to get people talking about the zany world of dolphin science. Luckily, there's no shortage of dolphin factoids to draw on since we're learning new things about dolphins all the time. Researchers are regularly discovering new dolphin abilities, new dolphin behaviors, and sometimes even new dolphin body parts. But before we begin, I need to point out a couple things.

First, we'd better get on the same page as to which animal(s) I am referring to when I write the word *dolphin*. There are over 35 species of dolphins living in the ocean today, with half a dozen more that live in rivers and estuaries. Some of them have clearly dolphin-sounding names, like the *dusky dolphin*, or the *Atlantic white-sided dolphin*. But some of them have wildly misleading names like the *melon-headed whale*, or the *killer whale*. The melon-headed whale is not actually a *whale*, and does not in fact have a melon for a head. There are a number of species of dolphins that have the word *whale* in their name – probably as a way of letting people know that they are really, really big. But melon-headed whales, just like killer whales, pilot whales, and false killer whales are all placed soundly within the Delphinidae family, making them fully-fledged dolphins. So don't be surprised when you start seeing the word *whale* bandied about in this book – I can assure you that all of the animals I am talking about in the following pages are in fact dolphins.

Second, there's a dirty little secret that you should know: science and scientists don't know everything. The thing about science is that our evidence-based ideas about how the world works are constantly being tested, refined, and in some cases completely overhauled. Some of the things we thought we knew about dolphins 50 years ago turned out to be wrong. And surely many of the things we think we know about them today will be found to be incorrect by future generations of scientists. This is a good thing. We need science moving forward, poking holes in our current theories so we can inch closer to the true nature of reality. As comedian Dara Ó Briain once said, "science knows it doesn't know everything; otherwise, it'd stop."

Since scientists are aware of how precarious their understanding of the world is, they often appear uncomfortable and squirmy during interviews. They try to avoid making concrete, definitive statements like "dolphins never chew their food." Scientists hate to use words like "never," and prefer saying things like "probably" or "usually" or "according to current findings." This is because there are often exceptions to any supposed rule about dolphin behavior. Perhaps there is a species of dolphin out there that does spend a lot of time chewing its food, but nobody has ever seen it. So instead of me filling this book with wishy-washy sounding statements about how little we really know about dolphin science, I will resort to easier to digest statements that are more fun to read. Honestly, sentences like "dolphins don't chew their food" are a lot easier on the eyes than "although scientists are still unsure as to the extent to which dolphins might or might not masticate when ingesting food due to limited dental samples and a paucity of behavioral observations for some species, the current body of evidence derived from tooth-anatomy and dental-wear in mature animals suggests that there is a high probability that food-chewing among delphinids is rare." Yuck! I guarantee that this book will be free from science double-talk along these lines, and filled with easy-to-digest information.

I've sorted these fantastical dolphin facts into four categories: 1) *Strange Behavior* (wherein we learn that dolphins do some pretty weird things), 2) *Impressive Skills* (wherein we learn that dolphins have unexpectedly awesome abilities), 3) *Bizarre Anatomy* (wherein we learn that dolphins' bodies can be very, very odd), and 4) *Messy Relationships* (wherein we learn that dolphins have complicated social lives). If there's one thing I have learned having spent years studying dolphins, it's that every time science uncovers a strange new dolphin ability or behavior, dolphins somehow become more mysterious and even more fascinating. I expect that you'll feel the same way after reading this book. So it's time now to dive into the following pages and see what unexpected dolphin-science treasures lie hidden below the waves.

Happy reading!

Justin

STRANGE BEHAVIOR

DOLPHINS DON'T DRINK WATER

Imagine for a moment that you are someone who loves dolphins with all of your heart. That there has never been another person on earth that has loved them more. You love them so much, in fact, that you want to spend the rest of your life living alongside dolphins in the ocean. Not in a cabin on the beach or on a sailboat, but actually in the ocean, swimming alongside your delphinid soulmates.

So you give away all of your earthly possessions, put on your favorite bathing suit and a lifejacket (to help you stay afloat while sleeping), and wade into the warm waters of Kealakekua Bay, Hawaii, where you hope to paddle alongside the spinner dolphins that live in the bay. You plan to hunt for food like the dolphins – catching fish and crustaceans, and eating the occasional mouthful of seaweed.

After a few hours of pure bliss swimming alongside your dolphin friends, you start to feel a bit thirsty. What do you do? Drink seawater perhaps?

Dolphins don't drink water

Terrible idea. Seawater contains a lot of salt. Salt is wonderful stuff, and your body needs salt to survive. But the concentration of salt in seawater is three times what it is in the human body. Which means that when you drink seawater, it will increase the salt concentration in your blood to abnormally high levels. This will have near immediate and catastrophic effects. Via the process of osmosis, the cells in your body will start losing water as they compensate for the difference in salt concentrations across the cell wall. Your kidneys will try very hard to remove and excrete all the excess salt, but they are unable to produce salt concentrations in urine that is higher than that of seawater. Which means that your body will begin to dehydrate as the salt from the seawater sucks all of the liquid from your cells.

Your dolphin friends, on the other hand, don't suffer from this problem. Their kidneys are a little better at removing salt from their blood, so it's possible for dolphins to ingest a bit more seawater than you without dehydrating. But they can't drink seawater either since their kidneys can't fully correct the osmosis problem. Only the sea otter has kidneys capable of producing urine with higher concentrations of salt than seawater, which means sea otters are the only mammal that can drink as much seawater as they want.

Twenty-Two Fantastical Facts about Dolphins

Unless you are a sea otter, don't drink seawater

So what then do dolphins drink? If you are going to live the rest of your life alongside dolphins, maybe you can just drink what they drink? Unfortunately, this isn't going to work for you. Dolphins get the water they need from the food that they eat. All of the yummy fish and squid and crabs that dolphins consume are filled with fresh water, and dolphins are able to extract and use this water to keep themselves hydrated. Humans, on the other hand, couldn't possibly get enough – let alone all – of the water they need from their food.

Dolphin skin is also designed to help them retain water – they do not sweat like humans, and don't lose as much water through their skin as we do. They might even be able to extract fresh water

Dolphins don't drink water

from the ocean through their skin. Thanks to a few anatomical changes to help them adapt to life in the ocean, dolphins simply don't need to drink in order to stay hydrated.

You, on the other hand, my dolphin-loving friend, cannot get the water you need from eating squid, or extract freshwater from the ocean via your skin. In fact, if you don't die from dehydration after spending too long bobbing in the ocean, it might just be your skin that kills you.

After just a few days of swimming in the ocean, you would probably start to develop skin sores and nasty bacterial and fungal infections. Human skin starts to break down after being submerged in water for days at a time. Even perfectly sterile water will destroy human skin if you stay in it for too long. And seawater is far from sterile.

What's worse, the constant water pressure will reduce circulation to your extremities. So your limbs will start to grow weaker, your heart and lungs will start working overtime, and eventually your skin will rot off. The take-home message here is that, unlike dolphins, humans did not evolve to spend extended periods of time in water. Dolphins might not need to drink in order to survive the desert-like conditions of the ocean, but humans certainly do.

So if you are going to spend a lot of time out in the open ocean with your dolphin friends, please be sure to bring something to drink. Or better yet: a boat.

DOLPHINS DON'T CHEW THEIR FOOD

What do sharks, alligators, dolphins, and my toddler all have in common? None of them chew their food properly. And in the case of the non-humans on this list, they don't chew their food at all.

Dolphins have a mouth full of teeth, but their teeth are designed to grasp food, not to tear it (like shark teeth) or crush it (like cow teeth). That's not to say that dolphin teeth aren't capable of ripping into flesh. The teeth-marks covering the bodies of most dolphin species are evidence of the less-than-innocent nature of dolphin teeth. Once a dolphin grabs hold of a potential meal, however, it's usually straight down the hatch without any chomping or chewing involved. Dolphin teeth are essentially a collection of enamel forks set inside a pair of chopstick-like jaws.

The obvious disadvantage of not having the ability to chew your food is that all the food you are about to swallow needs to be the right size. Since dolphins often hunt and consume prey that is quite a bit larger than can be swallowed in one go, they have developed strategies to help chunk up their food into manageable sizes. Bottlenose dolphins have been observed gnawing off and discarding the heads of oversized fish. This often means that the fish needs to be thrashed about a bit, or rubbed onto the ocean floor in order to rip it apart. A sort of tenderization process, but typically involving living fish that would prefer not to be tenderized.

Just slide it down the chute ma'am

Dolphins don't chew their food

Some dolphins have taken this tenderization process to a whole new level. One Indo-Pacific bottlenose dolphin in Shark Bay, Australia, developed a method for preparing cuttlefish – a dolphin delicacy – that gets around the problem of what to do with that inedible cuttlebone that takes up most of the animal's body. Instead of just eating the cuttlefish's head/face and calling it a day (which is what most dolphins would do), this crafty dolphin chef first squeezes and thrashes the cuttlefish (thus extracting all of the ink), and then brings it down to the seafloor where she pounds on it with her rostrum (beak) until the cuttlebone pops out.

Similar tenderizing techniques have been observed in killer whales, who are notorious for "playing" with their food. They fling seals about in the air, smack them with their flukes, and generally just pummel them into easier-to-manage pieces.

Dolphins also remove the tough flesh of fish, and even pluck out the spines from the pointier species before swallowing them. They aren't always so careful however, and plenty of dead dolphins have washed up on shore with fish spines lodged in their throats.

Unlike humans, dolphins don't really choke on oversized or spiny pieces of food. The pathway from their blowhole to their lungs is almost permanently separated from the pathway that leads from their mouths to their stomachs. The dolphin larynx has evolved into a funny-shaped piece of flesh called a goosebeak, which acts as a sturdy flap separating the airway from the digestive tract. When a dolphin "chokes" on something like a fishing net or an oversized fish, they are most likely still able to breath normally, but the debris lodged in their throat makes it impossible to eat.

In other words, you can't really perform a Heimlich maneuver on a dolphin. Instead, you can just reach down their throat and pull out the stuck item. Which is exactly what Bao Xishun – the world's tallest man (7 feet 8.95 inches) – had to do in order to save the life of a couple of dolphins in an aquarium in Fushun, China, that had swallowed large pieces of plastic. The plastic had become lodged in the stomach of the dolphins, and only the longest arm on the planet was able to reach down their throats and remove the debris. So let that be a lesson to any of you young dolphins out there: unless you happen to live down the road from the world's tallest human, be sure to take smaller bites.

DOLPHINS DON'T SLEEP

Almost all animals that live in the ocean are able to breathe water – extracting the life-giving oxygen that's swishing around in seawater with their gills. Crustaceans, fish, clams, amphibians – they all have gills, and don't need (and generally prefer to avoid) air. But marine mammals – which include dolphins, whales, seals, manatees, sea lions, otters and a handful of others – still need access to air in order to get their oxygen. The ancestors of all marine mammals were air-breathing land-animals, and during their millions-of-years-long return to the ocean, none of them bothered to evolve gills or other anatomical features that would allow them to stay submerged in water 100% of the time.

Thanks to the "whatever, that's good enough" attitude of evolution, dolphins are forced to stick their blowholes out of the water every few minutes in order to fill their lungs with oxygen-rich air. Some species can hold their breath longer than others, but most need to be at the surface a few dozen times every hour to breathe.

But if dolphins need to swim to the surface to breathe at regular intervals, how then do they ever get any sleep? Some species – like pilot whales – engage in behavior called logging where they float on the surface of the ocean with their blowholes above the waves. This seems a pretty logical way for a dolphin to sleep since it's able to keep its airway exposed at all times. But the thing is, most species of dolphin don't sleep at the surface like this.

In fact, dolphins don't really sleep at all.

When humans fall asleep, our conscious minds shut down, leaving the more primitive parts of the brain found in our brainstem – like the medulla oblongata – to take care of unconscious processes like breathing or making the heart beat. But the medulla oblongata in dolphins does not control their breathing. Dolphins must think about every breath they take using the parts of the brain that – in humans – is mostly shut off when we sleep. This means that dolphins need to remain conscious at all times or they simply stop breathing. In fact, if a dolphin ever does lose consciousness – like if you give it a general anesthetic – it will suffocate pretty quickly.

Luckily, dolphins have evolved a workaround. All animal brains must enter periods of sleep or restfulness in order to survive. Nobody is really sure why, but if an animal is denied sleep for long enough, it will die. Dolphins have found a way to get the rest they need by sleeping one half of their brain at a time. Dolphin brains, like all mammal brains, are divided into two hemispheres. Dolphins are able to shut down just one hemisphere at a time and enter into something called *unihemispheric slow-wave sleep*. This allows for one half of their brain to go offline while the other stays awake, so dolphins can continue swimming, watch for predators, and return to the surface to breathe with the awake part of their brain.

I've been awake for 8 years straight

Dolphins in this half-asleep mode usually swim lazily near the surface. Each half of the brain will sleep for a couple of hours before waking up and letting the other half get some shut-eye. And it really is shut-eye in most cases – you can usually tell which half of a dolphin's brain is asleep by looking at their eyes: the one connected to the sleeping half is shut while the other one is open. Dolphins often sleep like this at night time, and typically for about 8 hours per day – not unlike most humans. Well, except for the half-closed-eye thing.

Scientists have tested dolphins to see just how awake they really are when sleeping one half of their brain. In one experiment, dolphins were asked to touch a paddle every time they heard a tone. The tone was played at random every few minutes. Researchers kept producing the tones all day and all night for days at a time without the dolphins messing up, or even displaying signs of being tired. The experiment ended after 5 days, but probably could have been kept up forever. The dolphins, you see, weren't tired because they were able to sleep one half of their brain as needed, with the other half wide-awake and able to concentrate on the (really boring sounding) paddle task.

When it comes to staying awake and maintaining constant vigilance, it's dolphin mothers that are

Dolphins don't sleep

the true insomniacs. Newborn dolphins hitch a ride with mom by swimming right next to them, getting sucked into the wake that their mother's body creates while she swims through the water. If a dolphin calf positions itself in just the right spot next to mom, it will be propelled through the water without having to swim very hard, which helps it conserve energy. In order to make sure their newborns stay afloat and don't get too tuckered out, dolphin mothers need to keep swimming at all times in order to create this protective swim-bubble for their calves. Spend too much time logging near the surface, and their little ones might sink. So dolphin moms just keep swimming without a break for days/weeks/months until their calf is strong enough to handle the world on its own. They likely engage in unihemispheric slow-wave sleep at some point, but to the casual observer it looks like they don't sleep at all.

Based on my own experiences raising a human infant, this "total lack of sleep for months at a time" thing sounds pretty familiar...

DOLPHINS ALMOST NEVER DROWN

Being an air-breathing animal living in the ocean brings with it a number of challenges. Chief among them is trying not to drown. The paradox/problem of living in an aquatic environment but needing to be at the surface to breathe is something that manatees, sea turtles, whales, and dolphins have to cope with on a daily basis. But for dolphins, drowning in the traditional sense (which involves inhaling water into your lungs) is not really the problem.

Dolphins, you see, are sort of immune to drowning.

I know what you're thinking. This sounds like crazy nonsense. Don't hundreds of thousands of dolphins drown in fishing nets each year? Well yes, a huge number of dolphins are killed by fishing nets each year. But no, most dolphins trapped in nets don't drown.

They suffocate.

What's the difference? It all has to do with what's

happening with a dolphin's blowhole when they are trapped under water.

Dolphins are conscious breathers. This means that a dolphin must think about and decide on every breath it takes. Humans, in contrast, have the ability to let our brainstem take over the breathing duties, allowing us to continue to take breaths even when unconscious or asleep. Dolphins do not have this luxury.

This conscious-breathing setup means dolphins have evolved a strange relationship with their blowholes. A dolphin's blowhole – which is the only pathway to a dolphin's lungs – is closed by a sort of flap, which is attached to a very strong set of muscles. When closed, this flap creates a water-tight seal. The blowhole flap remains – by default – in the closed position. Below the blowhole are a series of internal flaps, valves, and other fleshy portals all of which create their own airtight seals – essentially creating four separate barriers between the outside air and a dolphin's lungs. So if a dolphin is just hanging about in the ocean not thinking about taking a breath, it doesn't have to worry about letting water into its lungs – the blowhole and other muscle-seals are tightly shut, and waiting on orders from the dolphin's conscious mind to open up and let in air.

This means that if a dolphin were to ever be knocked unconscious, he/she would sink to the seafloor, and come to rest at the bottom with their blowhole firmly shut. Should the dolphin fail to awaken before they run out of oxygen, they will die – not from drowning (that is, inhaling water), but from suffocation.

Something similar happens if a dolphin were to be trapped in a fishing net. Humans, when trapped under water and in desperate need of air, will almost always open their mouths and make one final, desperate attempt to breathe, sucking water into their lungs. It is rare for a human to suffocate under water without taking a final breath that fills their lungs with water.

A dolphin, on the other hand, is far less likely to inhale water this way. Although they might crave air just as desperately as a human, the blowhole and sphincter-seal system in their nasal cavity typically remains in the default, shut position.

Occasionally, dolphins that are sick might accidentally inhale water and drown if they are too weak to keep their heads above water. And some dolphins trapped in nets are so overcome by panic that they are able to override the seal-system and open their blowholes, allowing water into their lungs.

Dolphins almost never drown

Fishing nets are responsible for hundreds of thousands of dolphin deaths each year

But it is likely that most dolphins trapped in a net will ultimately succumb to suffocation as they run out of oxygen, and die with their blowhole closed. This is a terrible, if all too common fate for a dolphin, or any other air-breathing sea creature.

DOLPHINS BEACH, AND NOBODY KNOWS WHY

Certainly one of the saddest sights for anyone who loves dolphins is watching a group of these majestic animals lying helpless on a beach. Dolphins' sleek bodies are well-designed for zipping gracefully through the waves. But take them out of the ocean, and the thick layer of insulating blubber and muscle that keeps them warm quickly becomes an awkward, deadly straitjacket. If a dolphin spends too much time out of the water, its internal organs will be crushed under its own body weight. Breathing is especially difficult, and constant exposure to the sun will cause them to overheat. Thrashing about on the sand also leads to physical injuries, and the stress of the situation often sends their bodies into shock. It's rare for a dolphin to strand on a beach and actually survive. Land is really no place for a dolphin.

Why then do so many dolphins beach themselves?

In most cases when you find a single animal washed up on shore alive, chances are that animal is sick or dying. A dolphin that is too weak to swim might end up being washed onto shore by powerful waves. Or it might even decide to head to shallow waters where it can rest its body on the beach and keep its blowhole above water. It's a desperate measure to be sure, and will almost always lead to death, but when a dolphin is too weak to swim, it might be the only option.

Stranded false killer whales

Occasionally dolphins strand themselves on purpose while pursuing their prey. There are killer whales in Patagonia that chase seals up onto the beach, and bottlenose dolphins in South Carolina that herd fish onto muddy river banks. But these stranding experts rarely get stuck. The real mystery is why seemingly healthy dolphins sometimes strand together in huge groups. These mass strandings are very common – especially for species like pilot whales or false killer whales that don't usually spend a lot of time near shore.

Nobody is really sure why this happens. One of the most commonly cited theories is that the strong social bonds that dolphins forge cause them to follow their friends around wherever they go – even if they end up stuck on land. There are many cases of dolphins that appear to have followed a sick or dying companion into shallow waters, and refuse to leave their side – even as the tide goes out and they are left beached on dry land. The end result is that the entire group of dolphins perishes, not just the sick one. The group simply refuses to leave the side of their ill companion. There are many reports of humans trying to intercede in these situation and drag the healthy dolphins back out to sea. But their efforts are often wasted as these refloated animals swim right back onto the beach to be with their dying friend.

In some cases it appears as if the entire group is suffering from some sort of disease that causes them all to beach themselves at the same time.

Some mass strandings have been explained as a failure of the group to navigate shallow waters correctly. Perhaps something had been interfering with their vision or echolocation – like bubbles in the water, or a shoreline that slopes so gently that it looks like the open ocean. Or perhaps changes in the earth's magnetic field cause their internal compasses to receive incorrect positional information. Dolphins might navigate the open ocean using their magnetic sense, and fluctuations in the earth's magnetic field or magnetic material found near land can lead to confusion.

There is some evidence that mass strandings might be caused by human activity. The use of sonar by military organizations could very well be responsible for some stranding events. Loud sonar pings might frighten dolphins, sending them careening into shallow waters. It's also possible that deep diving dolphins might swim to the surface too quickly after being frightened by sonar, giving them the bends – a form of decompression sickness. Although dolphins were thought to be immune to the bends, there is growing evidence that this isn't the case. Loud sounds from sonar – or from any other human activity (like oil and gas exploration) could also damage dolphins' hearing, or cause other internal injuries that leave them susceptible to stranding.

Of course, traumatic underwater events that lead to strandings might not always be manmade. It's possible that natural seismic activity – like underwater earthquakes or volcanic eruptions – also cause dolphins to strand.

Whatever might be driving these groups toward the shore, there is one thing that many of these stranding events have in common: they are made a lot worse by the strong social bonds of the group. In so many cases, animals that have been rescued by humans and helped back out to sea will simply re-strand within minutes or hours in order to be with their friends. Which makes the tragedy of strandings even more tragic.

IMPRESSIVE SKILLS

DOLPHINS HAVE SUPER CRAZY HEALING POWERS

In September of 1989 a bottlenose dolphin nicknamed Freddy, who had been frequenting Warkwoth Harbour in Amble, England, was struck by a boat propeller. The corkscrewing blades sliced a series of 10 gashes into his flesh, cutting clean through the thick layer of blubber underneath his skin, and exposing the now damaged muscle tissue.

At the time of the injury, the town of Amble was pumping all of its domestic sewage directly into the harbor, which meant that Freddy's wounds were immediately exposed to E. Coli and other bacteria that could, at best, slow the healing process, but quite possibly kill him. Freddy, however, did not die. In fact, Freddy stopped bleeding almost immediately, and despite the infection that set in, his gruesome wounds completely healed within four months. Had Freddy been a human swimmer bathing untreated lacerations like these in sewage-tainted seawater, he would probably have been dead within a few days.

Dolphins have super crazy healing powers

Cases like Freddy's – where seemingly fatal wounds (typically shark bites) observed on wild dolphins simply close up and heal over like magic – are not uncommon. But this super-healing process is a mystery to science. To begin with, nobody knows how dolphins manage to clot so quickly – especially since they should be predisposed to clot more slowly than other mammals due to the way their circulatory system is designed to handle the pressure that comes with diving deep in the ocean.

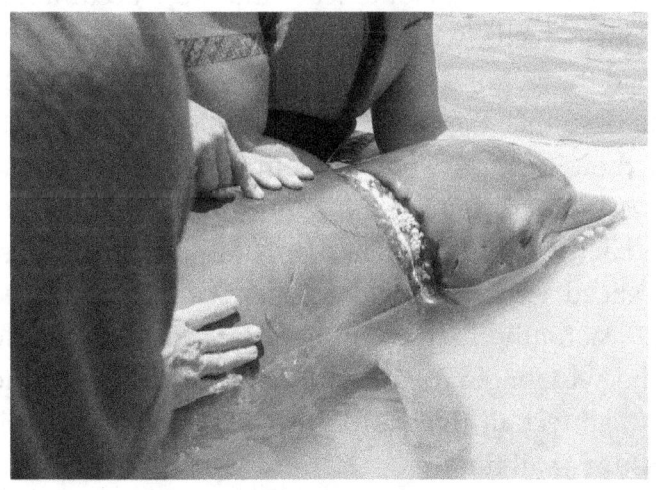

Looks nasty, but this dolphin made a full recovery

But what's perhaps most remarkable about their amazing healing powers is the ability to fight off infection. Seawater is filled with any number of species of microbial organisms and viruses that would consider an open wound the perfect location to reproduce with reckless abandon. And in Freddy's case, swimming through both seawater AND raw sewage with open wounds should have been fatal. So how did he manage to fight off infection?

The answer might reside in dolphins' blubber. Blubber, like most kinds of animal fat, has a tendency to store certain kinds of toxic compounds. For humans, chemicals like lead and DDT accumulate in our fat cells, which is generally considered to be a bad thing. For dolphins, however, it might well be the case that the dangerous chemicals they ingest in their food – whether from natural sources or from human pollution – wind up in their blubber and actually aid the healing process. When blubber is sliced open, these toxic chemicals are released and actually help kill the bacteria that would otherwise begin to grow in the wound. Like a kind of disinfectant that dolphins carry around in their tissues at all times.

But don't use this as an excuse to go dump a bucket of radioactive waste into the ocean in order to "help the dolphins heal." In all likelihood it's the naturally occurring fatty-acids produced by the dolphin's own body that is responsible for the infection-fighting that happens when a dolphin's flesh is cut open. Fatty acids are found in unusually high concentrations in dolphin blubber, and are thought to be used to lower the freezing point of their tissue, allowing them to swim through frigid waters without turning into dolphin-popsicles. But acids are also good at killing bacteria, which might explain how Freddy managed to swim through an E. Coli bath without any ill effects.

Regardless of how they do it, dolphins seem to have an uncanny ability to recover from flesh wounds. Since as many as half the dolphins in any given population will have shark-bite scars on their bodies, and almost all of them will receive scrapes and cuts from (play) fights with other dolphins, having quick-healing skin is key to surviving life in the ocean.

DOLPHINS USE TOOLS

It was the year 1835; a year of discovery. It was in this year that Charles Darwin visited the Galápagos Islands for the first time aboard the HMS Beagle, setting him on a path that would lead to his theory of natural selection. It was the year that European pioneers arrived at the base of the Yarra River in Australia and signed a treaty with the local Aboriginal people, establishing the city of Melbourne. It was in this year that, 2,000 miles to the west of Melbourne in a shallow bay known by locals as Gathaagudu, a lone female Indo-Pacific spotted bottlenose dolphin made a discovery that would alter the course of dolphin history forever: she learned to use tools.

The dolphins of Shark Bay, Australia (formerly Gathaagudu), are now world famous for their crafty use of marine sponges as tools. Scientists first discovered this behavior in the 1990s when they spotted a handful of dolphins swimming with sponges clamped onto their rostrums. There are all sorts of sharp objects and spiny, venomous animals hiding in the sand that could poke the dolphin's

Dolphins use tools

unprotected (and very sensitive) rostrum, so the dolphins use sponges as a kind of shield to protect themselves while burying their faces in the sand to pull out tasty treats.

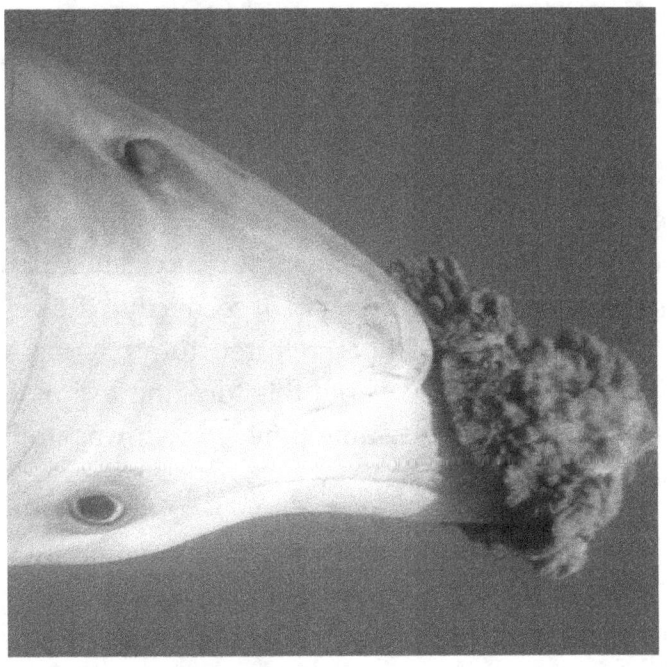

A dolphin carrying a marine sponge

Not all of the dolphins in Shark Bay use sponges in this way. Only a small group of around 60 animals – known as the spongers – forage for food like this. And almost all of them are female.

The sponging technique appears to be something that is passed down from mother to daughter, although some males do engage in sponging as well. Young dolphins learn how to forage with sponges by watching their mothers, and they in turn appear to model the behavior for their own offspring. The passing down of a learned behavior through the generations like this is referred to as *culture* in animals.

Because sponging is really only performed by a few dozen dolphins in Shark Bay, we can make an educated guess as to exactly how many generations back the behavior first began. It seems that the very first sponging dolphin – referred to as Sponging Eve – probably discovered this foraging technique 180 years ago; at the same time Darwin was in the Galápagos.

The question remains as to how Sponging Eve figured out the technique. Did she stumble across it by accident after getting a sponge stuck on her rostrum? Did she hit upon the idea via a flash of insight after ruminating on the problem of how to dig up fish without getting stabbed in the face? It's almost impossible to know for sure. However she came up with the discovery, it appears that Shark Bay is the only place on earth where dolphins have learned to use tools in this manner. Which makes Sponging Eve a true dolphin pioneer.

DOLPHINS CARRY WEAPONS

Psychologists have learned that holding an otherwise innocent object in your hand – like an umbrella – makes onlookers perceive you as more dangerous than if you were empty-handed. This same, subconscious fear of weapon-like objects is lodged in the minds of many of our primate cousins. Our closest relatives – chimpanzees – appeal to this weapon-fear bias by waving tree branches and logs in the air when trying to make themselves look larger and more intimidating. And by golly it works. As anyone who has spent time in the African jungles can attest to, a giant male chimpanzee screaming and running at you with a tree-branch in his hands is full-on terrifying. This is one of the reasons I prefer to study dolphins. They don't have hands, so the chances they will club me or my fellow researchers to death in the open ocean are small.

Or so I thought.

It now appears that dolphins are known to wield weapons too. The Amazon river dolphin – also called the *boto* – has been observed carrying tree branches in its mouth. Since these river-bound dolphins live quite close to vegetation, it's easy enough for them to get their ~~hands~~ mouths on weapon-like objects. They have been observed jutting their heads out of the water and waving sticks or branches around – a lot like chimpanzees.

Why do botos do this? Nobody has witnessed them actually assaulting other botos with their makeshift weapons, so it's probably not meant as a tool to punish rivals. Then again, chimpanzees usually don't hit each other with sticks – they just brandish them as a means of looking tougher. This is probably what is happening with the botos as well. It's almost always the males who engage in this stick-thrashing behavior, and almost always when they're around other males. Most of the time, these stick-carrying bouts end in some sort of aggressive encounter between the males. Tail slaps, biting, ramming – all kinds of unfriendly dolphin stuff.

Unsurprisingly, stick-wielding is often witnessed at times of the year when the females are most fertile. So it seems likely that males are trying to impress the ladies or otherwise scare their rivals

Dolphins carry weapons

by carrying weapon-like objects in their mouths. It might well be that the male dolphin who carries the biggest stick also has the best luck when it comes to mating.

Watch out! This boto has a leaf!

Carrying sticks or other objects is an awkward thing for a dolphin to be doing. It will slow them down as they swim, and make it impossible to eat. Like much of dolphin behavior, it's still a mystery as to why they do this. But I can guarantee you that a giant male Amazon river dolphin charging at me with a stick in its mouth is enough to keep me from wanting to swim in the Amazon. Well, that and the piranha.

DOLPHINS FIGHT IN HUMAN WARS

Human divers are a total joke when it comes to looking cool under water. They are painfully slow, and the SCUBA equipment they need to carry around with them in order to simply not die is comically cumbersome. They lug huge air tanks on their backs, stuff their mouths with awkward breathing devices, and plaster oversized masks to their heads. Diving deeper than just a few meters means that things go haywire with gases in their blood, forcing them to stop swimming and just bob around in the water every once and a while to let their bodies acclimate to changes in water pressure. Only James Bond has ever managed to look suave while engaged in underwater action scenes. And that was thanks to the magic of cinema.

If, however, you are in the market for graceful underwater warriors in real life, look no further than the dolphin. They rarely suffer from any of this decompression sickness nonsense, and can zip through the water at astonishing speed. Their graceful underwater acrobatics make SCUBA divers look like waterlogged Twinkies.

It's for these reasons that dolphins have been used in military operations around the globe for over half a century. US military scientists were fascinated by dolphins' efficient swimming abilities, and skill at holding their breath, so began studying them in the 1950s to see how they might make military vessels (and divers) more dolphin-like. Dolphins' echolocation systems also received a lot of attention and directly contributed to military (and civilian) knowledge of sonar. The military soon figured out that dolphins were quite clever – very good at taking instructions and carrying out complex tasks. It did not take long to connect the dots and realize that dolphins could be used to conduct complex underwater military tasks. And so the U.S. Navy Marine Mammal Program was born in the 1960s.

This program was kept super-secret for many decades, only being declassified in the 1990s. Dolphins, as well as other marine mammals like seals, were trained to seek out and tag underwater mines, and were deployed in Vietnam and the Gulf Wars where they patrolled the waters near US ships. It has been long rumored that some of these dolphins were even trained in anti-personnel tactics – taught to kill enemy divers. The US Navy has denied such shenanigans, however.

Perhaps not surprisingly, the Soviet navy began their own military dolphin program in 1965. During the Cold War, both the Soviets and the Americans were in a sort of dolphin arms (flippers?) race to see who could create the ideal dolphin solider. With their powerful echolocation skills that could work in murky or even pitch-black water, it was simply impossible for navy frogmen to replicate the dolphins' skill at exploring and navigating an underwater environment.

Dolphins were fitted with mine detecting and tagging gear, dropped from helicopters, taught to jump up and ride along on small military boats, retrieve lost items, escort ships, carry surveillance equipment, and so on. They were also quite useful for rescuing humans floundering in the water. If the rumors are to be believed, some of them were even fitted with explosive darts that could kill enemy divers; it's likely that the Soviet dolphins at least were provided this kind of deadly training. Given the Soviet Union's notoriously secretive society, it is still a mystery as to what sorts of weird things they got up to with their dolphins in the infamous Area 75 near their naval base in Sevastopol.

Dolphins fight in human wars

A dolphin from the U.S. Navy Marine Mammal Program

These days, the Soviet military is no more, and their former military dolphins are used for friendly dolphin-swim sessions in the Black Sea. Although with Russia's relatively recent annexation of Crimea and its dolphin training facility, these former military dolphins might be pressed back into service. The US is phasing out its military dolphin program after finally having developed technology that almost rivals the echolocation and underwater navigation skills of their dolphins. It's a testament to how sophisticated dolphins' abilities are that it took the military more than half a century of study and many hundreds of millions of dollars to finally reach a stage where human technology (just might) approach the dolphins' natural skillset.

DOLPHINS SENSE MAGNETIC FIELDS

Do you know how they say that toilet water in the southern hemisphere swirls in the opposite direction to toilet water in the northern hemisphere when you flush? It turns out that that's a myth. For toilet water anyway.

Dolphins living in the southern hemisphere, on the other hand, do swirl backwards. Well, not so much swirl backwards in a toilet bowl as swim backwards in a pool.

People noticed this phenomenon a few years ago when watching the swimming patterns of captive dolphins in South Africa compared to captive dolphins in Europe. The European dolphins spent most of their time swimming in a counterclockwise direction in their pools, whereas South African dolphins swam clockwise. Nobody is sure why this happens, but it might have something to do with the earth's magnetic field.

The outer core of the Earth is comprised of liquid iron that swirls around producing a magnetic field. Like the two poles of a magnet, the fields extend in opposite directions in the northern and southern hemispheres. Scientists suspect that if dolphins can sense these magnetic fields, it might somehow be affecting their swimming patterns.

Many animals are sensitive to magnetic fields. Pigeons use these fields to navigate, and dogs appear to use them to poop. For reasons only they can know, dogs tend to align themselves along the north-south axis of the earth's magnetic field when doing their business.

Only very recently were scientists able to confirm that dolphins too are able to sense magnetics fields.

But how do they do this? Dolphins and other animals are able to feel the magnetic pull of the Earth when it tugs on miniature deposits of magnetite, a substance embedded in their brains.

Magnetite is a mineral comprised of strongly magnetic iron oxide that forms miniature crystals in the brains of a number of species, from bacteria to humans. These crystals are sensitive enough to react to the relatively weak magnetic field of the earth.

Being able to sense the earth's magnetic field is extremely useful for a dolphin. Because the global magnetic field is relatively stable, and forms a

Dolphins sense magnetic fields

Magnetite is found in small quantities in the brains of dolphins

kind of patchwork of loops and swirls, dolphins are likely able to memorize its structural patterns in much the same way you or I would memorize the layout of the grocery store. For those dolphin species that spend all of their time in the middle of the vast ocean where there are no physical structures to tell them where they are, the magnetic fields might be the only landmark they'll ever encounter. For a species like the pilot whale, which spends most of its life floating dozens of miles above the seafloor and hundreds of miles from the nearest landmass, neither their echolocation nor their vision is any use for telling them where they are. It's up to the magnetite in their brains to give them the information they need to find their favorite fishing grounds.

If dolphins really are reliant on the magnetic field for navigation, then this might help to explain why some species beach themselves. Subtle changes to the patterns of Earth's magnetic field occur regularly, and the fields can be bent or misshapen by landmasses that contain iron or other magnetic minerals. Deepwater dolphin species tend to get stuck on beaches that overlap with magnetic fields that don't correctly match up with the layout of the shore. It might be that strange magnetic anomalies are giving the dolphins conflicting information about where the shore is located, so they wind up disoriented and eventually stranded on a beach that the magnetite in their brains is telling them isn't there.

We're still trying to figure out how big a role these magnetic fields play in dolphins' lives. Just because they can sense these fields does not necessarily mean that they actually make use of them. Humans, after all, can sense magnetic fields too and this doesn't appear to affect our behavior. Although it might be worth asking someone in Australia which direction they prefer to swim in – clockwise or counter-clockwise. If they say "clockwise," you can tell them it's probably because they have rocks in their head.

DOLPHINS CAN SEE YOUR BONES

Dolphins have a kind of x-ray machine built right into their heads. It's not exactly as powerful as the human-made x-ray generators used to take pictures of broken bones in a hospital, but it does have the ability to penetrate soft material – like sand, or even flesh.

Here is how this marvel of evolutionary engineering works. Dolphins produce clicking sounds using the vocal apparatus in their heads. These clicking sounds occur in a rapid series, resulting in something called a click train or echolocation train. It sounds a lot like a creaky door in an old haunted house being slowly opened.

The sound waves created by these clicks are shot out of the front of the dolphin's head, passing straight through that big fatty structure on the front of their head which is called a *melon*. Dolphins can change the shape of their melon to focus this beam of echolocation sound waves, a bit like a flashlight. The sound waves then travel out into the water where they bounce off objects in the dolphin's environment.

If, for example, a click bounces off a rock, it will produce a click echo which then travels back to the dolphin. The dolphin listens for each of the echoes coming back. By listening to changes in the echoes (for example, changes in the volume of certain frequencies) the dolphin is able to build up a mental image of the object. This audio image can be just as detailed as the visual image humans see using our eyes.

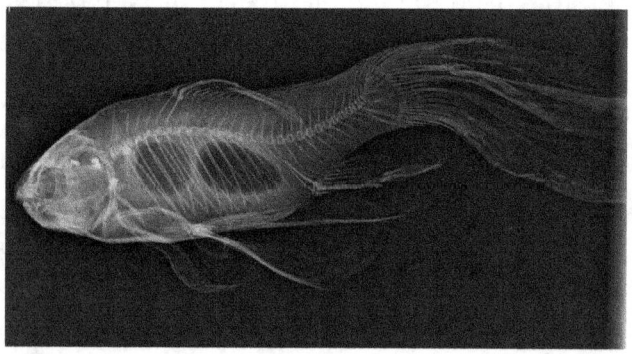

I just totally x-rayed your goldfish with my head

This might sound pretty bizarre, but humans do something similar. If you are able to hear, you might be surprised to learn that you use your ears to hear objects (like walls) that are around you. If you plug your ears and spend a day walking around, you will notice that you bump into things more often – because you've lost your ability to hear obstacles in your environment. Some visually impaired people have learned to produce their own click sounds just like a dolphin, and they listen to the echoes to hear where they are going – they can ride a bike while clicking, and even hear things like a credit card resting on a table.

But dolphins have evolved crazy-sensitive echolocation, and are able to hear much more information about objects in their environment than a clicking human. The really wacky thing about this process is what happens when these echolocation clicks encounter an object made of soft material.

A really hard object – like a rock – is pretty much 100% reflective. But something soft – like sand – allows some of the energy from the sound waves to penetrate it. So if a fish is buried in the sand, a dolphin can echolocate on the sand and sound waves will bounce back off the bones or air bladder of the fish, allowing the dolphin to essentially see through the sand with its echolocation clicks to find the fish. And these clicks will also penetrate the fish's body allowing the dolphin to see some of the internal structure of the fish. Some of the sound will bounce off the skin, but some of it will penetrate through and bounce off bones, teeth, organs, etc. In this way, a dolphin can get a "sound image" of the entire fish, seeing through it somewhat like Superman's x-ray vision.

DOLPHINS CAN HEAR EACH OTHER'S THOUGHTS

Consider how strange your life would be if whenever you stood within a few feet of another person, you were able to see whatever it was they were looking at. Not because you both happened to be facing the same direction, but because your friend's visual field was magically projected in your mind's eye. For example: if your friend was sitting next to you on the couch watching Lord of the Rings on the iPad while you were watching Star Wars on TV, you would constantly see mental images of Gandalf and hobbits and elves superimposed over Darth Vader and Luke and Han Solo. Whatever your friend was seeing, you'd be seeing too.

This kind of scenario might be hard to imagine for us humans, but it's the everyday reality for dolphins. Not through the sense of vision, but through echolocation.

To understand how this weird ability comes about, it's important to come to grips with how echolocation works. For a dolphin, the sense of echolocation is every bit as powerful as their sense of vision when it comes to producing a mental image of the world around them. Instead of light waves bouncing off of objects and being translated into visual information by their retinas, dolphins can bounce sound waves (in the form of echolocation clicks) off of objects and use their ears to produce mental images of their environments.

These echolocation clicks provide information about whatever objects they bounce off of – be it a fish, a human swimmer, or the rocks, sand, and reefs that surround them. The information about these objects made available to dolphins via sound waves contains similar levels of detail to what is available to them via their visual system. It is, in a way, the ability to see with sound.

Echolocation is intended to be a closed, private system; designed for the benefit of the dolphin doing the echolocating, and not anyone else.

But, and this is where things get strange, if a second dolphin happens to be swimming close to his friend who is busy echolocating on an object (like a mackerel), the listening dolphin – who is not producing any echolocation of its own mind you – just might hear some of the returning click echoes. This creates a scenario where the listening dolphin will be able to hear exactly what that mackerel looks like thanks to his friend's echolocation. And, bizarrely, the listening dolphin will be able to "see" the mackerel whether he wants to or not. Simply being in the vicinity of a friend using echolocation on a fish means that dolphins close enough will have the mental image of a fish projected into their mind.

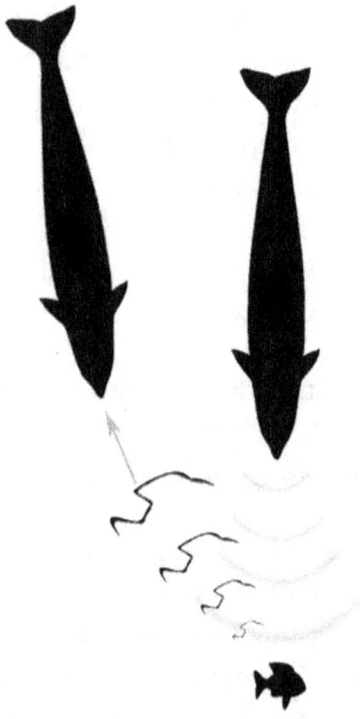

The dolphin on the left can "hear" the fish
thanks to the dolphin on the right's echolocation

Dolphins can hear each other's thoughts

It might well be that the ability to eavesdrop on your friend's echolocation like this could yield scenarios where dolphins either take advantage of or try to avoid each other's echolocation. Imagine again how different life would be if we were constantly bombarded by the images other people were seeing whenever you were close to them. Teachers would always know whenever students were secretly watching Star Wars on their smartphones instead of paying attention in class. Although they seem to have this ability anyway. Perhaps most teachers are actually dolphins?

BIZARRE ANATOMY

DOLPHINS HAVE EARS IN THEIR JAWS

Whales and dolphins evolved from furry mammals with hoof-like feet that roamed the Earth 50 million years ago. Called Pakicetus, these animals looked like a cross between a dog, a cat, and a tiny, angry hippopotamus. They walked on four legs, had a snout with eyes on the front of their heads, and sported cute little gerbil-like ears.

As natural selection began the process of transforming Pakicetus into the modern-day dolphin, the ancestors of dolphins lost many anatomical features that weren't helpful to them in their new aquatic environment. They traded in their body hair for a thick layer of blubber to help keep them warm. Their gangly limbs were transformed into sleek flippers and flukes – far more useful for propelling them through the water. And those cute little gerbil-ears – which would have slowed them down in the water – disappeared altogether.

Dolphins have ears in their jaws

Pakicetus

The visible part of Pakicetus' external ear – that floppy little pancake that most extinct and living mammal species have on the sides or tops of their heads (including humans) – is called an *auricle* or *pinna*. It acts almost like a satellite dish that amplifies sound and directs it toward the ear hole. If you look closely at the side of a dolphin's head, you can still see a tiny pin-prick where their ear hole is, but the pinna itself is completely gone.

But it wasn't just the pinna that underwent a radical change as Pakicetus evolved. The strangest transformation took place under the hood. The tiny ear hole seen in modern dolphins, which originally transported sound waves to the middle or inner ear, no longer serves any purpose at all. Dolphins' ear canals are completely blocked up with fibrous tissue, ear wax, and other fleshy debris. Sound is no longer able to make its way from a dolphin's ear hole to its inner ear.

How then do dolphins hear at all? This was a question that stumped scientists back in the 1940s when they first began examining dolphins' hearing anatomy. Dolphins clearly have very sensitive hearing, and are able to detect sounds at extremely high frequencies, well beyond what a human or even a dog could hear. But how were dolphins transporting sounds from the outside world into their inner ears if they had blocked-up ear canals?

It turns out that all the work that used to be done by the pinna – amplifying sound and directing it to a dolphin's inner ears – is now done by a dolphin's lower jaw. A dolphin's jaw is filled with a kind of fatty substance that leads directly up into their middle ear. As sound waves travel through the water, they are absorbed by the dolphin's jaw and are directed up along this fatty canal. With a jaw bone on each side of its head, a dolphin is able to use its jaws much like we would use pinna on the sides of our head – allowing them to pinpoint where a sound is coming from. And since the fat in their jaws is similar in density to water, this allows sound waves to travel easily to their inner ears.

This fancy new lower-jaw hearing system is made extra effective with the help of dolphins' teeth. The more-or-less evenly spaced rows of 22 teeth that dolphins have in each jaw actually help them to amplify sound. Their teeth act a bit like an antenna, with the teeth resonating at frequencies that dolphins use for their echolocation. This hearing system likely evolved in tandem with dolphins' echolocation ability.

Lady, get your fingers out of my ear

Although dolphins might have lost their cute gerbil-ears, they appear to have traded them in for some rather sophisticated auditory technology. It's yet another bizarre feature of an animal that has taken a rather unorthodox evolutionary path.

DOLPHINS SOMETIMES HAVE BACKWARD DORSAL FINS

Spinner dolphins are pretty bizarre as far as dolphins go. Their habit of leaping out of the water and spinning around at high velocity is just odd – not something other species of dolphins usually do. It's made even more bizarre by the fact that nobody knows why they do it. It might be to shake off pesky suckerfish that are latched onto their sensitive skin. Or maybe it's a form of communication, or a mating display. Or, as is likely the case for lots of dolphin behavior, it's just something fun to do.

It's not just that spinner dolphins act strange. They also look strange. An adult male spinner dolphin typically has a huge bump just behind its genital area called a ventral hump. The older a male dolphin is, the bigger its hump. So what's in the hump? Nothing important really – mostly connective tissue. And what's the point of a hump? Like many weird anatomical structures seen only on males of a species (like moose antlers or peacock tails), its sole purpose is to advertise how strong/

awesome the male is, which both intimidates rivals and attracts the lady dolphins. Some other species of dolphins, like common dolphins, also grow a little hump for similar purposes. But nothing rivals the size and prominence of an adult male spinner dolphin's crazy-looking hump.

Adult male spinner dolphins also have an impossibly strange-looking dorsal fin. It looks exactly like it's been stuck on backwards. Instead of the fin curving from front to back – like you see in almost all other dolphin, shark, and fish species – it curves towards the front. As the males age, their dorsal fins change shape. When they are young calves, their fins are the normal size and shape. But once they reach full maturity, the fin loses its backwards curve and looks more like a triangle. As they continue to age, it starts pitching forward.

Male spinner dolphin

So what's going on here? Probably more of the same "check me out ladies" kind of shenanigans that you find with their ventral humps. It might be the case that a backwards fin makes it harder to swim, so if an adult male can still manage to be at the top of his game with this kind of physical "handicap," then other males know to leave this tough-guy alone. And the ladies will know that he's probably good dad-material. Female spinner dolphins also have a reverse-fin sometimes, so it's not just a male thing.

Male spinner dolphins also have odd-looking upturned or curled tail flukes. This might be yet another anatomical oddity that is meant to attract the ladies. Or it might help them swim faster. Nobody knows. Bottom line: adult male spinner dolphins look like they've been crafted out of playdough by a toddler who has no idea what a dolphin should look like.

DOLPHINS COMMUNICATE WITH THEIR NOSTRILS

Pakicetus, the ancient land-dwelling ancestor of dolphins, had a long snout full of teeth with two little nostrils on the end of it. A bit like a wolf's snout. Over the course of millions of years, these dolphins-to-be evolved to spend more time living and hunting in the water. Having nostrils at the front of their snouts became a rather annoying inconvenience since they'd need to position their heads awkwardly above the water to take a breath. It was far easier for an air-breathing, water-dwelling creature to have their breathing holes on the top of their heads, and dolphins were lucky enough to evolve just such a solution. And so, their wolf-like nostrils migrated to the top of their heads. And then things got weird.

Unlike their baleen whale cousins (like the humpback or blue whale), dolphins have just a single blowhole on the top of their head, which is how they suck in air. Baleen whales have two holes – looking like a pair of nostrils – and that's more or less exactly what they are. But the dolphins' dual-nostril system didn't stay on their heads (like that of baleen whales), nor did it morph into the single blowhole that we see today. Instead, the nostrils migrated into the middle of their heads, and the single-blowhole – a brand new structure – evolved on top of them. Their two nostrils, now buried deep in their heads, are no longer involved in smelling, or in keeping their airway shut at all; that's the job of the blowhole. Instead, what's left of the dolphins' nostrils are used exclusively for communication.

A dolphin's blowhole consists of a single opening

Dolphins communicate with their nostrils

Dolphins' former nostrils evolved to look like a pair of funky lips that are able to flap back and forth, vibrating rapidly enough to make sounds that they use to communicate with each other. By passing air over these phonic lips – between the air pockets and air sacs in their heads – they can make both whistle and click sounds. They're so dexterous when it comes to manipulating their phonic lips that they can make whistle sounds with one set of lips while, at the same time, making click sounds with the other. In fact, some species of dolphins have a dedicated set of click-lips and another set of whistle-lips.

It was really only in recent years that scientists figured out how dolphins were even able to make sounds. It first seemed logical that the dolphin was whistling by passing air across its blowhole – like you or I would do when passing air over our lips to whistle. But the blowhole isn't used to make sound at all. And neither is the larynx – the hollow tube that, for humans, houses our vocal cords. Dolphins have a larynx, but no vocal cords. No, it's the phonic lips – the ancient dolphin nostrils – that they are using to make all those adorable dolphin sounds.

DOLPHINS ARE COVERED IN SCARS

Dolphins have a nasty habit of chewing on each other. Whether it's part of an innocent game where they try to grab their friend's pectoral fin, or it's an aggressive encounter where they violently bite their rivals on the face, dolphins are constantly sinking their teeth into each other. Since dolphins don't have hands, claws, or paws, the only option they have for grabbing onto things is mouths. And since dolphin mouths are filled with dolphin teeth, visible bite marks on the skin of their friends (and enemies) wind up being pretty common.

If you check out the skin of most species of wild dolphin, you will notice all sorts of scars and bite marks. You will often see a relatively shallow set of white parallel marks that look like the dolphin was swiped by the claws of a werewolf. These are called tooth rake marks, a result of being grazed by the teeth of another dolphin, and can be found on most species. Typically, it's the males that are sporting the greatest number of tooth rake marks since most dolphin males are keen on getting into bitey fights. Tooth rake marks are fairly shallow – healing relatively quickly – a result of a play-bite as opposed to a serious chomp-attack.

But looking at the body of species like Risso's dolphins, you'll notice that these poor souls are simply covered in nasty tooth rakes. Risso's dolphins are supposed to be gray in color, but the number of bite-marks on their skin gives them the appearance of being white. And poor old Amazon river dolphins are also covered in bite marks and scars. In fact, Amazon river dolphins – which are sometimes called pink dolphins – are pink because their skin gets so covered in scar tissue from being chewed on by other river dolphins that their skin turns a pale red color. Adult male river dolphins are almost entirely covered in scar tissue – pink when they should be (in their natural, un-chewed-on condition) gray.

A Risso's dolphin covered in tooth rake marks

It gets nastier though. Most dolphins carry around the scars of failed shark attacks – those telltale half-moon bite-marks. And a lot of species bear the scars of a particularly nasty kind of shark called the cookie cutter shark. These little sharks live in deep waters and have a set of sharp teeth that allow them to carve out a round chunk of flesh from any dolphin that swims across its path. It's actually a rather clever trick: the dolphin almost never dies from the cookie cutter bite, meaning that the dolphin swims away to live another day, and to provide another meal to the next shark. Like a swimming buffet.

It might not be fatal, but a cookie cutter bite is no picnic. It penetrates through the blubber and into a dolphin's sensitive muscle tissue. Cookie cutter sharks are powerful little biters – they've even been known to take bites out of the hulls of submarines. Once the scar heals, it will leave a distinctive round scar. You often see young dolphins that are free from scars – having avoided aggressive encounters with other dolphins or sharks for the first few weeks of their lives. But wait a few decades and any baby-skinned calf will have grown into a weather-beaten adult that will more than likely be covered in scars.

DOLPHINS ARE HARD TO COUNT

How many species of dolphin are there? Seems like a pretty straightforward question. But it's not. There isn't really an answer. There is no institution that oversees the classification of animal species, so it's up to individual experts to make the final call. The problem is, each individual scientist has her/his own opinion. And they rarely agree with each other.

You can – and often do – have a whole room full of dolphin experts debating for hours, without any consensus, as to whether different populations of dolphin that otherwise look identical are in fact the same species. There are a variety of methods experts use to tell one species from another – you can do this based on the structure of their bodies, the structure of their genes, where they live, or even how they behave. With such a variety of methods, it's no wonder nobody can agree.

Consider the following example: the bottlenose dolphin. This sounds like a pretty easy to recognize, single dolphin species, right?

Twenty-Two Fantastical Facts about Dolphins

Nope.

To begin with, people often refer to the Indo-Pacific bottlenose dolphin (those dolphins found in Shark Bay, Australia) as simply a bottlenose dolphin. But this species, which is indeed in the genus *Tursiops* alongside common bottlenose dolphins (*Tursiops truncatus*), is given the species name *aduncus*: they are officially *Tursiops aduncus*. Indo-Pacific bottlenose dolphins are quite different from the common bottlenose dolphin in that they are smaller, fatter, with a longer rostrum, and develop spots on their bellies. In fact, genetic evidence suggests that they are far more closely related to the genus *Stenella* (which includes spinner and spotted dolphins) than common bottlenose dolphins.

People have long tried to split the common bottlenose dolphin into different species, including the Pacific bottlenose (*Tursiops gillii* – which most scientists these days simply refer to as *Tursiops truncatus*), the South American bottlenose dolphin (*Tursiops nesarnack catalania* – which is now understood to be *Tursiops aduncus*), and the Black Sea bottlenose (*Tursiops truncatus ponticus*). The Black Sea dolphin is considered by some to be a subspecies of the common bottlenose dolphin (that is, a population of animals that live in a unique area separate from the rest of their species). Many scientists, however, don't acknowledge Black Sea dolphins as a subspecies either, and refer to them simply as common bottlenose dolphins.

A group of researchers published an article in 2011 arguing that we should split off a new species of bottlenose dolphin in Australia – called the Burrunan dolphin – into its own species (*Tursiops australis*). Of course, not everyone agreed with them, so many people don't use this new name.

A Burrunan dolphin. Or is it?

To make matters more confusing, there are different ecotypes of the same species of common bottlenose dolphins, with some scientists arguing that perhaps these too should be split into different species. This includes a larger, darker bottlenose dolphin that lives further from shore (called the offshore ecotype), and the regular version that most people are familiar with (called the nearshore ecotype). These two ecotypes rarely mix – even when present in overlapping habitats, but are probably not dissimilar enough to be granted different species status. Well, depending on whom you ask.

Once geneticists and taxonomists start looking at all of the different kinds of bottlenose dolphins found throughout the world, it's possible to start lumping or splitting them in all sorts of madcap ways. Often what happens is a group of scientists publish an article proposing a new species of dolphin (like the Burrunan dolphin) which the scientific community then evaluates and debates. Sometimes scientists will start using the new name for the new proposed species, but other scientists – who disagree – still use the old name. There are local, national, and international agencies that decide to adopt a new species (or not) for reasons of conservation or research, and these often dictate what is "officially" a new species. What is "official" is a bit in the eye of the beholder, however.

In the meantime, and while all of this arguing continues, we'll just have to accept that scientists don't really know how many species of dolphin there are. And probably never will.

MESSY RELATIONSHIPS

DOLPHINS KILL THEIR OWN CALVES

Infanticide. It's a nasty business. Unfortunately, the act of killing young animals of the same species is all too prevalent in the animal kingdom. Lions are famous for their cub-killing proclivities. When a new adult male takes over a pride, he sometimes kills all the cubs that were sired by his former rivals.

Dolphins too are likely involved in infanticide. I say "likely" because, despite thousands of hours of observation, proof that male dolphins kill dolphin calves of the same species is still lacking. The circumstantial evidence, however, is pretty darn strong.

Consider this gruesome incident that took place a few years ago. In the Moray Firth in Scotland, an adult male bottlenose dolphin was seen darting into a group of male and female dolphins, and later emerged with a young calf gripped in his jaws. Pursued by others in the group – including the calf's mother – the male attacked the young dolphin, ramming and butting him, pushing him to the seafloor, and tossing him out of the water with violent force. Eventually the attack ended with the near lifeless calf draped motionless across his mother's back. Miraculously, the calf survived, only to die 8 months later. Was the calf's death a result of the male's aggressive behavior? Possibly. Probably in fact. If so, then this might well be a case of dolphin infanticide. Or at least attempted infanticide.

A bottlenose dolphin calf/potential victim

What exactly is this kind of behavior all about? Why would a male dolphin want to kill another dolphin of the same species? Like most of the weird behavior observed in the animal kingdom, it's a result of complicated male-female relationships. Male bottlenose dolphins are, like most male animals, deeply concerned with passing on their genetic material. A male that is looking to sire some offspring with a female dolphin that is busy raising a young calf is going to be out of luck. Dolphin mothers of young calves will not be interested in getting pregnant again for a while. One of the solutions to this "problem" is for the male to kill the calf, leaving the mother with no option but to seek out a new father for her next calf. If the male kills the calf of a female he has not mated with in a while, he can be fairly certain that he didn't just kill his own offspring. If he then sticks around for a few months and waits for that female to come back into heat (and hopes she forgets all about his calf-killing character flaw), then his infanticidal tendencies have just increased his chances of becoming a father himself.

Female dolphins obviously are not down with infanticide, and don't want to subject their calves to this kind of violence. And so the constant threat of infanticide might be one of the factors driving the evolution of dolphin society – the reason that males and females hang out in same-sex groups a lot of the time.

It's not really fair to suggest that male dolphins are always keen on calf-killing though, or that dolphin societies are structured around the females' attempts to prevent infanticide. In most cases, males and females get along just fine. But infanticide probably

Dolphins kill their own calves

is an issue that some dolphins do encounter. Which is a serious bummer. It's hard being a dolphin calf out there in the great big ocean; the last thing you need is some giant male dolphin trying to kill you in order to mate with you mom.

DOLPHINS OFTEN DIE YOUNG

In June of 2015, a gruesome photograph of a half-eaten baby dolphin was posted on Facebook, and promptly incited global panic. The calf's body had washed up on a beach in Wildwood, New Jersey, and bore the telltale signs of having been ravaged by sharks. A half-moon bite-mark occupied the space where the calf's belly should have been, and its tail had been ripped off. Many online commenters rushed to the conclusion that the coast of New Jersey was now infested with ruthless, dolphin-killing sharks.

In all likelihood, however, this young dolphin had not been killed by a shark. Sharks prefer to scavenge the bodies of dead animals as opposed to wasting energy trying to hunt down and kill speedy little critters like dolphins. This young dolphin would have been long dead by the time a shark began nibbling on it.

Was there another killer lurking off the coast that was responsible for the dolphin's death? Indeed there is a likely candidate, but it's not an animal that would strike fear in the hearts of most New

Jersey beachgoers. Based on what we know about mortality in newborn dolphins, the animal most likely responsible for this young calf's death was in fact the calf's own mother. Not because she actively killed her offspring, but because she didn't have the necessary parenting skills to keep him alive.

You call 'em calves, I call 'em hors d'oeuvres

Dolphins, like humans, spend the first few years of their lives dependent upon adults for almost everything. They are unable to forage for food themselves, and are reliant upon their mother's milk for nutrients. For dolphins, it's the calf's mother that does the lion's share of work, with occasional help from other female dolphins. The mother is responsible for protecting the dolphin from predators – like sharks or infanticidal male dolphins. But her main job, and the one that often flummoxes new dolphin mothers, is being able to feed her offspring. It's the mother's ability to provide adequate nutrition for herself and her young calf that is the key to the calf's survival. This is, it would seem, no easy task given that up to 50% of newborn dolphins will die before they reach their first birthday. The vast majority of these are not killed by sharks, but are victims of their mother's inability to find enough food.

It's a mystery as to why some dolphin mothers are more successful than others. It might be that first-time dolphin mothers are simply not skilled or experienced hunters, and are unable to consume the necessary calories to keep their bodies in good enough condition to produce adequate milk for their calves. Or it might be that mothers that are social outcasts lack the kind of support network of other female dolphins that they need. Without a team of responsible adults to help babysit the young calf when the mother is off foraging, a mother might find it impossible to be an effective hunter with a newborn dolphin in tow. Or perhaps a dolphin mother that had a calf at a very young age simply hasn't yet learned what she needs to know to be an effective parent. Dolphins learn many skills by watching other members of their social group, so the more exposure a young mother has to the good-parenting techniques of her peers, the better her chances of being a successful mother.

Older dolphins, who have more knowledge of good foraging spots and the best methods for keeping calves out of harm's way, tend to make the best mothers or babysitters. The benefits of having older female dolphins in the group who are able to pass on this kind of knowledge is likely why some species of dolphins (including pilot whales and killer whales) are one of the few animal species on earth that survive long past the age where they are able to have offspring of their own. These grandmother dolphins are able to pass on their knowledge and skills to the next generation of mothers.

Although we can never be sure what the cause of death was for the half-eaten dolphin calf that washed up on the beaches of Wildwood, New Jersey, it is very unlikely that this otherwise healthy young calf was chased down and mauled by a hungry shark. Without a sufficiently skilled mother or watchful grandmother to look out for him, this young dolphin probably starved to death long before he became a shark's dinner.

DOLPHINS NEVER LEAVE THEIR FRIEND'S SIDE

Do you have that one amazing friend who you can tell all your secrets to? The one you get in touch with whenever anything noteworthy happens in your life? You probably talk to them every day, go on vacation together, and generally try to spend as much time together as you can.

OK, so now imagine how life would be if you spent not just a lot of time, but every single waking moment with this person. I mean EVERY moment. You sit within two feet of them at every meal, stand next to them in the shower, and hold their hand each time they use the toilet. Imagine that you were never out of each other's sight. And what if you shared each other's personal space like this for, let's say, 40 years?

Well, that's more or less what's it's like for some male bottlenose dolphins living in Shark Bay, Australia.

Dolphins never leave their friend's side

In some dolphin societies, strong friendships form between two (or more) male dolphins. Occasionally, these friendships last for the two animals' entire lives. They are about as intimate as you can get in the animal kingdom, with the unrelated males swimming in close proximity to each other throughout their lives.

This is my brotha from anotha blubba

Why do these males form these tight bonds? It's probably partly because they like each other, but also for a much more practical purpose: it helps them get the ladies.

That's right, it's those messy male-female relationships that are driving yet another bizarre dolphin behavior. These strong male friendships –

called *alliances* – are formed to help the males gang up on females when it comes time to mate. In a behavior called *herding*, male alliance members will chase after a female, separate her from a group, and keep her all to themselves. These herding incidents aren't always violent, and the female is sometimes perfectly happy with the whole arrangement, so it's by no means always a sinister scenario. Having one or two male buddies by your side certainly increases the male's chances of fathering a new calf once the female is ready to mate.

It's during this herding phase when it helps to have a few friends on hand. A group of male dolphins is better equipped to chase off other males that are threatening to persuade the female to join them. And by sticking together, they can follow the female around to make sure she doesn't run off before it's time to start making calves.

Unfortunately, like most things in dolphin society, these social groupings tend to get complicated. Male groups sometimes join forces with other male groups to form *second order alliances*; creating a larger combo-group that can chase off the first group. If this first group isn't happy about this, they might join forces with yet another group to take back their females. And sometimes these two-group combos form alliances with other two-group combos creating *third order alliances* – gangs teamed up with other gangs teamed up with other gangs – all vying for the attention of the female, and sometimes getting into all out brawls. Several dozen of these multi-group alliances have been seen fighting in Shark Bay. Unlike most animal species that form complex groups (like chimpanzees), dolphins are not in it to defend their territory. It's really all about herding the females.

Each of the male dolphins in these groups is, in most cases, out for himself, which means that group membership changes as individuals betray their (second and third order) alliance members in search of stronger team-members. The whole thing can turn into a soap opera of epic proportions, and you need a wall-sized flow chart just to keep track of who is allied with whom.

But at the core of this tangled social mess you often find two male dolphins – a pair of friends that spend every waking moment together.

DOLPHINS EAT EACH OTHER

There are over 35 species of dolphin in the world, and most of them eat fish, crustaceans, and other food items that you might typically find on the menu at a sushi restaurant. But there is one species of dolphin that has gone seriously off-menu and seemingly developed a taste for its own kind: the killer whale.

Killer whales (also called orca), the largest dolphin species, occasionally hunt down and consume some of their dolphin brethren – smaller dolphin species like bottlenose dolphins or white-sided dolphins. But not all killer whales do this. In fact, most killer whales would never consider eating another dolphin.

Killer whales come in a variety of forms called types or ecotypes. The three different types of killer whale inhabiting the northern Pacific Ocean are referred two as transients, residents, and offshore types. Although they all look similar enough, it's possible to distinguish these three types based on differences in the white patches around their eyes

Dolphins eat each other

and behind their dorsal fins, and the size and the shape of the fins themselves. But it's their diets that really set them apart.

Residents typically eat salmon and other fish, and spend most of their time near shore looking for their prey. Offshore types spend most of their time in the open ocean eating large fish and maybe even sharks. But transients don't really care all that much for fish. They eat – exclusively – the flesh of other marine mammals. This includes seals, sea lions, porpoises, and baleen whales like minke or grey whales. It's these transient types that have been known to hunt down, kill, and eat other dolphin species.

Sure, Flipper's my cousin, but he's also delicious

The internet is filled with video evidence of this orca-on-dolphin violence. Tourists on cruise ships and whale watching vessels off the west coast of the US and Canada have documented many examples of transient killer whales pursuing, incapacitating, eating, and sometimes even playing with their (doomed) dolphin prey.

Mammal-eating killer whales and fish-eating killer whales rarely bump into each other when foraging in the ocean – due in large part to their polar opposite dietary choices. Transients and residents appear to live their lives in completely isolated worlds, separated not only by their choice in food, but by their choice in social partners. Despite sharing the same exact habitat, they avoid all social contact with each other, and there has probably not been a case of transients and residents getting together to mate in tens of thousands of years.

Their hunting styles are also quite distinct. Because most marine mammals have excellent hearing, transients usually hunt their prey in total silence. The dolphin and porpoise species that they are targeting could easily hear the orcas' clicks and whistles, so radio silence is essential for tracking down and killing species with excellent hearing – like the bottlenose dolphin.

Dolphins eat each other

This orcas-eating-dolphins scenario is not exactly cannibalism in that killer whales don't eat other killer whales. But transients, in any case, don't seem to have a problem with eating their closest delphinid cousins.

DOLPHINS CALL EACH OTHER BY NAME

Lots of different animal species are able to recognize their friends and family members by the sounds of their voices. Penguin colonies consist of thousands of noisy birds, with hundreds of baby penguins making honking noises in hopes that their mothers will recognize and find them in the crowd. And they usually do. Even humans can pull off this trick: if your mother, your best friend, and President Obama were all to sing the same version of "Somewhere Over the Rainbow" to you over the phone, you'd have no trouble telling who was who based solely on the quality of their voice. So this skill isn't such a big deal in the animal kingdom really.

But what is a big deal is being able to recognize who someone is by their name, not their voice. If I say "hello, my name is Frank Drebin" to you, it doesn't matter if I have a cold, disguise my voice using one of those weird FBI witness-protection filter things, or speak to you using Stephen Hawking's voice generating computer. The fact that I use a unique name – Frank Drebin – means that you know who I am. And this is exactly how dolphins are able to recognize each other; a trait seen in humans and dolphins but no other animal species.

This is how it works. After a dolphin is just born, it will hear the whistles of all the other dolphins around it, including its mother or any friends and relatives that are nearby. If it's a captive dolphin, it might also hear the whistles from its trainers. Dolphin whistles sound, to a human, a lot like a human whistle, going up and down in tone. Throughout the first months of a young dolphin's life, it will take all this whistle information on board, and eventually create a new whistle-call of its own from the bits and pieces of the whistles it's been exposed to. It will use this new, unique whistle call as a kind of contact call, announcing its presence, or repeating its whistle when it is stressed, lost, or sick. This unique whistle is referred to as a *signature whistle*, and will remain quite stable throughout the dolphin's life. So stable in fact that scientists (and other dolphins) can use this unique whistle as a way of identifying the individual using it. A bit like a name.

Each dolphin will have its own signature whistle – sometimes resembling the whistle of its mother, but sometimes resembling other sounds it hears in its environment. Some dolphin calves even base their signature whistle on the sound of a trainer's whistle. Occasionally, dolphins that spend a lot of time together will start forming a new whistle together – based on each other's whistles.

"Flipper" was most certainly not his real name

Dolphins might call out each other's whistles – possibly as a means of getting the attention of a specific friend. A dolphin's ability to remember which whistle-name belongs to which dolphin, and to maybe even use another dolphin's whistle-name, is a rare trait in the animal kingdom. Of course, not all species of dolphins are known to have a signature whistle, and some species don't make whistle sounds at all. But these non-whistling dolphins might recognize each other based on unique structures to their clicks. In dolphin society, being able to tell the difference between individuals based just on their signature whistles (or click structure) is obviously important. What's even cooler: dolphins, unlike most species, retain the ability both to learn and produce brand new whistles throughout their lives. So if you ever meet a dolphin out in the ocean, be sure to whistle your name. Your new dolphin friend just might remember it and whistle it back to you someday.

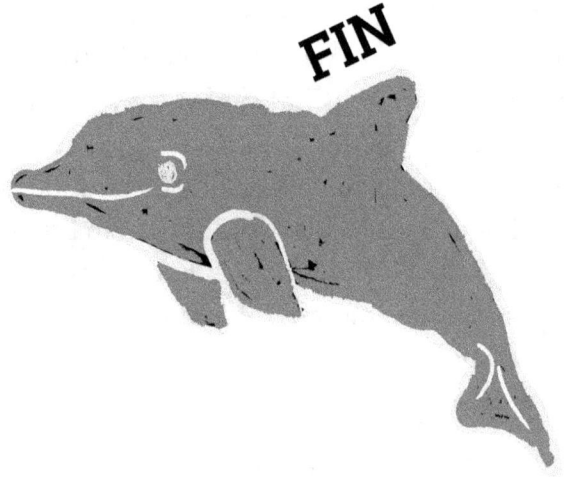

ABOUT THE AUTHOR

Justin Gregg, PhD, is a Senior Research Associate with the Dolphin Communication Project, and Adjunct Professor at St. Francis Xavier University. He is the author of *Are Dolphins Really Smart?*, published by Oxford University Press. He has spent many years studying dolphins around the world and currently lives happily with his family among the wildlife in rural Nova Scotia.

DID YOU ENJOY THIS BOOK?

If you'd like to help bring more books like this into the world, then please consider following Outside the Lines Press' three-step plan for reader awesomeness:

1) Tell a friend about this book! Tweet it, post it, spray-paint it – whatever your preferred method of sharing your thoughts.

2) Rate or review this book on the book-review-website of your choice – like Goodreads or Amazon.

3) Join the Outside the Lines Press mailing list. You'll get an exclusive peek at upcoming book projects, book giveaways, and general awesome information about generally awesome books. Here's the link: tinyurl.com/TheBestMailingListEver

Outside the Lines Press is a small, family-run independent press and there's nothing we like better than interacting with our readers. So keep in touch.

WWW.OUTSIDETHELINESPRESS.COM

IMAGE CREDITS

Page 10: Gregory "Slobirdr" Smith https://www.flickr.com/photos/slobirdr/15800171602 (http://creativecommons.org/licenses/by-sa/2.0)]

Page 14: Dolphin's dinner, by Zemlinki! (https://www.flickr.com/photos/zemlinki/256675975) (http://creativecommons.org/licenses/by-sa/2.0)]

Page 27: by Bahnfrend (Own work) (http://creativecommons.org/licenses/by-sa/3.0), via Wikimedia Commons

Page 35: NOAA News Archive 070208; by Georgia Department of Natural Resources

Page 39: from Patterson EM, Mann J (2011) The Ecological Conditions That Favor Tool Use and Innovation in Wild Bottlenose Dolphins (Tursiops sp.). PLoS ONE 6(7): e22243. doi:10.1371/journal.pone.0022243

Page 43: by Michelle Bender (http://www.flickr.com/photos/-mbender/5354172843/) (http://creativecommons.org/licenses/by-sa/2.0), via Wikimedia Commons

Page 51: by Norbert Kaiser (English: own work. Deutsch: eigene Aufnahme.) (http://creativecommons.org/licenses/by-sa/2.5), via Wikimedia Commons

Page 54: Angelo's X-ray, by John Smith (https://www.flickr.com/photos/61287964@N00/6083485009) (http://creativecommons.org/licenses/by-sa/2.0)

Page 63: by Nobu Tamura (http://spinops.blogspot.com) (Own work) [GFDL (http://www.gnu.org/copyleft/fdl.html) or CC BY 3.0 (http://creativecommons.org/licenses/by/3.0)], via Wikimedia Commons

Page 65: by Dolphin Discovery (https://www.flickr.com/photos/dolphindiscovery/2556562143) (http://creativecommons.org/licenses/by-sa/2.0)]

Page 73: by Citron / CC-BY-SA-3.0, via Wikimedia Commons

Page 77: from Charlton-Robb, K. et al. (2011) A New Dolphin Species, the Burrunan Dolphin *Tursiops australis* sp. nov., Endemic to Southern Australian Coastal Waters PLoS ONE 6(9): doi: 10.1371/journal.pone.0024047

Page 83: by Dolphin Communication Project/Kelly Sweeting

Page 87: by Hermanus Backpackers (Great White Shark Cage Diving) (http://creativecommons.org/licenses/by/2.0), via Wikimedia Commons

Page 91: by Peter J. Markham; https://www.flickr.com/photos/pmarkham/5753797602 (http://creativecommons.org/licenses/by-sa/2.0)

Page 95: by Christopher Michel (http://creativecommons.org/licenses/by/2.0), via Wikimedia Commons

All other images are public domain

www.ingramcontent.com/pod-product-compliance
Lightning Source LLC
Chambersburg PA
CBHW050542300426
44113CB00012B/2223